LUXURY IN YOU

LUXURY IN YOU

MOZA-BELLA

New Life Clarity Publishing

205 West 300 South, Brigham City, Utah 84302
http://newlifeclarity.com/

The Right of Moza-Bella to be identified as the
Author of the work has been asserted by her in accordance
with the Copyright Act 1988.

New Life Clarity Publishing
name has been established by NLCP.

All Rights Reserved.
No part of this publication may be reproduced, distributed, or
transmitted in any form or by any means, including
photocopying, recording, or other electronic or
mechanical methods without the prior and express
written permission of the author or publisher, except in
the case of brief quotations embodied in critical reviews
and certain other noncommercial uses permitted by
copyright law.

Printed in the United States of America

Copyright@2023 Moza-Bella

DEDICATION

This book is dedicated to my beloved parents. Without your love and guidance, I would not be where I am today. Your selfless sacrifice and unconditional love have been a forever-loving source of inspiration and motivation for my growth. I love you so much.

To all the women who have sacrificed your own dreams and aspirations to care for others, this book is dedicated to you, and to all the dreams you have put on hold. I hope that this book will serve as a reminder that you deserve to live a life full of joy, fulfillment, and happiness. Let's experience the Freedom of Luxury - the Luxury of being YOU.

FOREWORD

Throughout our lives, we each have the experience of meeting remarkable individuals who help to reshape our thoughts and heighten our reflective insights on achieving our goals.

I met Moza at a business conference several years ago. I was immediately impressed with her sophisticated professionalism. Since that time, we have become close friends.

Over the years, I've learned of her upbringing in Vietnam. She was a young ballerina who studied and performed this classical art form for 15 years. Immersing herself in such fine art since the age of 7 certainly shaped her subconscious mind to appreciate the fine detail, discipline, poise, and grace.

After immigrating to the United States in her early twenties, she put herself through school earning her masters degree, and then nursing degree years after. Having achieved these scholastic goals primarily on her own is a true testament to her personal drive and perseverance.

Thriving to achieve her goals remotely from her family, overcoming hardships mainly on her own, Moza has developed a profound understanding of love and compassion for others.

She has accumulated enriched experiences in various fields including entrepreneurial, medical, governmental , educational, corporate, hospitality, etc. She has an authentic desire and devotion to help other professional women to experience the Luxury of revealing their greatest-self.

I know without question that she brings a special energy into this world that makes everyone in her presence feel inspired and empowered.

While enjoying the pages of this book, you will also acknowledge that Moza truly wants to help you find the Luxury of being YOU.

Erikk Peterson
Vice President
Nordic Forge Incorporated

Dear Luxurious

The true meaning of Luxury involves great comfort, elegance, and refinement. My only hope as I was writing this book is to see you shine beautifully, elegantly, and confidently wherever you go.

The travel journal is for you to reflect on your own experiences. I would love to hear all about them. Share with me at moza@moza-bella.com, or you can always send me a message on my social media.

Your beauty and happiness start from within. Be a life-long learner, enrich your heart with respect and kindness, refine your appearance with elegance and poise, and you'll see the most Luxury has always been in YOU.

Moza-Bella

TABLE OF CONTENTS

- Dedication v
- Foreword vii

- Introduction 1
- Dress like a lady! 6
- Air Travel 8
- Traveling by Water 11
- Sports Events 29
- Household Daily 32
- Dining Adventures 39
- Special Events 46
- About The Author 106

INTRODUCTION

Nervous, anxious, fearful of embarrassing herself in front of the other guests and host, the girl was unable to engage in the conversation. Too many pieces of shiny silverware and sparkling glasses on the table, precisely placed in front of her seat, her heart was pounding in her chest, her hands were sweaty, and she felt so small in the ivory satin chair. That poor pathetic girl was the 14-year-old me.

I was invited to have dinner with the Japanese Ambassador and his wife. When I first arrived, stepping out of the old yellow taxi, my eyes scanned the magnificent white building of the Japanese Embassy. My little finger touched the doorbell, a man in a black suit walked earnestly towards the gate, gently smiled and bowed as I nervously took my first step into the premises. I remember how graceful and kind the Ambassador and his wife were to myself and the other guests throughout the entire evening. After dinner, they asked their daughter to play the piano for us. I did not know if I should clap, or sing along, or say a few words, or just be quiet and sip on the tea. I was never taught how to behave at a diplomatic dinner.

Years went by, growing as a female professional, I found myself attending press conferences, formal dining events, private club gatherings and corporate functions. Every time I entered a new social environment, my emotions instantly reminded me of the embarrassment I encountered when I was 14. I could not stand that crippling sensation. I had to fix it.

I started to learn about formal etiquette, which gave me the ease and confidence at formal events. However, since I started traveling around the world, I realized that what was considered socially acceptable in one region could be detrimentally impolite in another cultural occasion. Learning and practicing proper etiquette is equally important in showing your respect to others, presenting yourself with poise, elegance, and confidence, and to make people feel comfortable being around you.

I have met and worked with thousands of professional women, some of them choose to be with me in my mentoring programs to discover the ultimate Luxury in themselves and to experience the freedom of Luxury (and no, it is not about the price tags). Proper etiquette in every situation and every culture separates the refined sophisticated ladies from those who lack these skills.

MOZA-BELLA

The best experience that my ladies have shared with me is their feelings of empowerment when they walk into the room and own it. A stylish, classy, professional woman will definitely take the conversation to the next level.

This etiquette journal is the product of over 30 years of my personal and professional experiences. I want to share with you what has helped me feel comfortable in any situation, from a friend's home party to a private dinner at a Billionaire's mansion, from a polo event to a private yacht gathering. My hope is to see you shine beautifully and elegantly wherever you go. Remember to take this journal with you to keep the memories of your thoughts and feelings as you are preparing for your next travel experience and/or upcoming events.

I also recommend that you take another copy for your best friend, maybe another one for your sister, or whomever you'd like to see flourish on their journey of enjoying the Luxury in their gorgeous-self.

Additionally, if you happen to have a 14-year-old daughter, please hand this journal to her and share my life-lessons. She needs the guidance from you to build her confidence, so she can gracefully shine and be well respected wherever she goes.

LUXURY IN YOU

How to experience Luxury when Traveling?

Choose the right destination: The location of your vacation can significantly impact the experience you have. Choose a destination that offers luxurious accommodations, dining, and activities.

Use luxury travel services: Luxury travel services such as private transportation, personal concierge, and luxury tour agents can help enhance your travel experiences.

Stay at a luxury hotel or resort that offers amenities such as spas, fine dining, and personalized services to enhance your experience.

Book exclusive experiences: Luxury experiences such as private tours, wine tastings, helicopter rides, horseback riding, etc can add an extra element of luxury to your trip.

Enjoy fine dining: Indulge in gourmet cuisine at Michelin-starred restaurants or other high-end dining establishments. Pay attention to the fine details to fully appreciate the cuisine arts.

Relax at a spa: Book a spa treatment or spend a day at a spa to relax and rejuvenate. You may want to enjoy hot stone massages, facials, hydrotherapy, etc., just to name a few.

Dress the part: Dressing up in luxury attire will help enhance your experience. Pack elegant clothing and accessories that will make you feel elegant and fabulous.

Smile and leave gratuity: be kind and courteous to the service staff, and they will often go above and beyond to make your stay as luxurious as possible.

Take advantage of exclusive perks: Many luxury hotels and resorts offer exclusive benefits such as access to private beaches, pools, and clubs. Take advantage of these to make the most of your luxury experience.

Embrace the moment: most importantly, remember to embrace the moment and enjoy every aspect of your luxury experience. Savor the food, appreciate the service, enjoy the scenery, and take in all the luxury around you.

DRESS LIKE A LADY!

If you would like to present yourself as an elegant, sophisticated lady, then you should stay away from these clothing items, especially at formal gatherings:

- **Jeans and shorts**
- **Athletic wear or overly tight outfits**
- **Sneakers, flip-flops, or sandals**
- **T-shirts and tank tops**
- **Overly revealing or provocative clothing**
- **Hats and caps** - Unless the event specifically calls for a hat or cap, it's best to avoid them altogether.

———

Etiquette is all about showing consideration and respect to others. By keeping these tips in mind, you can ensure that everyone has a pleasant and enjoyable experience in your presence.

———

Daily Etiquette Tips

- Say "please" and "thank you" whenever appropriate.
- Use proper table manners when eating with others.
- Hold doors open for others and let people exit elevators or trains before entering.
- Avoid interrupting others when they are speaking.
- Always greet people with a smile and a positive attitude.
- Dress appropriately for the occasion or event.
- Be punctual and arrive on time.
- Use your indoor voice when speaking in public places.
- Keep your phone on silent or vibrate in social situations.
- When attending an event, bring a small gift or offering for the host or hostess.
- Use proper language and avoid using profanity or offensive language.
- Listen actively when others are speaking and show interest in their thoughts and feelings.
- Be respectful of others' personal space and belongings.
- Avoid gossiping or speaking negatively about others.
- Say, "Excuse me" when you need to pass someone or when you need to leave a conversation.

AIR TRAVEL

A few years ago, I was on my way to Florida from Chicago. There is a man in the aisle seat, and a woman in the window seat. Not long after I sat down in the middle, I realized they are together, unpleasantly expressing their obvious irritation that the middle seat now occupied. They talked to each other loudly, handed things over my seat - and across my face. The woman brought her own food, when she opened the bag; the smell was overwhelmingly circulating throughout the entire section. I wished someone had told her a few simple things NOT to do when traveling.

Air Travel Etiquette

1. When choosing a seat, avoid taking up more than your allotted space. Keep your belongings stowed under your seat or in the overhead compartment to minimize clutter.
2. If you struggle to lift your luggage over your shoulders, check it in, do not carry it on the airplane then expect someone else to do it for you.
3. Wipe down the sink in the lavatory and leave it in better condition than you found it.
4. Keep your voice down when engaging in conversations.
5. Never put your belongings in someone else's overhead bin or underneath someone else's seat
6. Avoid grabbing the back of someone else's headrest when you get up or sit down.

Flight Private Etiquette

Private flights are different from commercial flights, simply because they usually involve a smaller number of passengers.

Be punctual: Private flights often run on a tight schedule, so it is essential to arrive on time or even a little early to avoid delaying the flight.

Be mindful of luggage: Private planes usually have limited space for luggage, it is important to pack only what you need and follow any weight restrictions.

LUXURY IN YOU

Be considerate of other passengers: If you are traveling with other passengers, be mindful of their personal space and avoid loud conversations or music that may disturb them.

Respect the crew: Private flights typically have a smaller crew, and they are often very attentive to each individual's needs. Treat them with respect and follow their instructions.

Communicate your needs: Private flights can be customized to your specific needs, but you need to communicate them to the crew beforehand to ensure they can accommodate you.

Clean up after yourself: do not forget to clean up after yourself and avoid leaving any mess or garbage behind.

Alcohol and drugs: Private flights often have strict rules regarding alcohol and drug use, so it is important to avoid consuming them unless explicitly allowed by the crew.

―――

TRAVELING BY WATER

One time, I was on a yacht for a business gathering. There was a woman speaking on the phone on and off all day. Her voice was so loud; I thought everyone could hear her conversations. She had quite a few drinks, walking constantly from one deck to another with heavy footsteps.

Yacht etiquette is an important part of yachting culture and demonstrates your understanding of the proper protocol for yacht travel. It shows you value and appreciate the privilege of being on a yacht and are treating the experience with the utmost respect and care. Following yacht etiquette can make the experience more comfortable for everyone onboard.

Yacht Etiquette

Respect the captain and crew: The captain and crew are in charge of the yacht, and their decisions should be respected at all times. They are there to ensure your safety and enjoyment, so it is important to treat them with respect.

Follow the dress code: Some yachts have a dress code for certain areas, such as the dining room. Make sure you follow the dress code and dress appropriately for the occasion.

Be punctual: Yacht schedules can be tight, so make sure you are on time for all activities and events. If you are running late, notify the captain or crew as soon as possible.

Keep the yacht clean: keep it clean and tidy. Do not leave personal belongings lying around or cluttering up the common areas.

Be mindful of other guests: Remember that you are sharing the yacht with other guests, so be considerate of their needs and preferences. Avoid being loud or disruptive. Respect their privacy and preference of personal space.

Follow safety guidelines: Familiarize yourself with the yacht's safety guidelines and follow them at all times. This includes wearing appropriate safety equipment when required and following emergency procedures.

Tip the crew: Yacht crews work hard to ensure your experience is enjoyable, so it is customary to leave gratuity at the end of the trip. The amount of gratuity will depend on the size of the yacht and the level of service provided.

Boating Etiquette

Boating etiquette refers to the set of unwritten rules and practices that should be observed by boaters to ensure safe, enjoyable, and respectful experiences for everyone on the water.

Follow the rules of the waterway: Always follow the established navigation rules and laws for the waterway you are on. These include speed limits, no-wake zones, and right-of-way rules.

Keep a safe distance: The distance will depend on the speed of the boat and the waterway conditions. Maintain a safe distance from other boats, obstacles, and swimmers.

Avoid creating wakes: Reduce speed and avoid creating wakes when passing other boats, kayaks, canoes, or paddleboards. Large wakes can cause damage to other boats and can be dangerous to smaller vessels.

Use caution near shorelines: Slow down near shorelines, docks, and marinas to avoid disturbing wildlife, people fishing, and other boats.

LUXURY IN YOU

Avoid drinking and boating: Do not drink alcohol or take drugs while operating a boat. These impair your judgment and reaction time, making boating more dangerous.

Do not litter: Keep the waterways clean by properly disposing of trash and avoiding littering. Simply pack out what you bring in.

Be considerate of others: Keep music and noise at a reasonable level. Be mindful of other boaters, swimmers, and wildlife. Do not disturb wildlife or enter restricted areas.

Be prepared for emergencies: Have a working radio, life jackets, first aid kit, and other safety equipment on board.

Follow docking and anchoring etiquette: Avoid blocking access to other boats or impeding their movement. Be considerate when docking or anchoring near other boats.

Take a boating safety course: Take a boating safety course to learn more about boating rules and safety procedures.

―――

International Cultural Etiquette

Since I started traveling around the world, I realized what is considered socially acceptable in one region could be detrimentally impolite in another cultural occasion. Learning and practicing proper etiquette is equally important in showing your respect to others. In presenting yourself with poise, elegance, and confidence, you will make people feel comfortable being around you.

———

Chinese Etiquette

Chinese etiquette is a set of social norms and customs that have been passed down through generations in China:

Respect for elders: In Chinese culture, elders are highly respected, and it is important to show them deference and to address them properly.

Gift giving: Gift giving is an important part of Chinese culture, especially during festivals and important occasions. It is customary to bring a small gift when visiting someone's home.

Dining etiquette: it is important to wait for the host to take the first bite before eating, and to use chopsticks properly.

Communication: Chinese communication etiquette emphasizes politeness and indirectness. It is important to avoid being confrontational or aggressive when speaking with others.

Dress code: Dressing appropriately is important in Chinese culture, especially when attending formal events or visiting religious sites.

Business etiquette: In business settings, it shows respect to exchange business cards, and to use formal titles when addressing others.

Taboos: There are several taboos in Chinese culture, including avoiding the number four, which is associated with death, and never gifting clocks, which sounds similar to the word for "funeral" in Chinese.

Vietnamese Etiquette

Vietnamese etiquette is profoundly influenced by Confucianism and emphasizes respect for hierarchy, family, and social harmony.

Greetings: In Vietnamese culture, it is common to greet with a friendly smile, especially those who are older or in higher positions. A common greeting is "Xin chào" (pronounced "sin chow"), which means "hello". When meeting someone for the first time, it is polite to address them using their title and full name.

Bowing: When greeting someone who is significantly older or of higher status, it is customary to bow slightly as a sign of respect. This is especially important when you are meeting someone's parents or grandparents.

Removing shoes: Vietnamese remove their shoes before entering someone's home or certain public spaces, such as temples or pagodas. Look for a shoe rack or ask if you should remove your shoes before entering someone's house.

Table manners: Vietnamese people typically eat with chopsticks and a spoon. It is considered impolite to use chopsticks to point or gesture. It is also customary to wait for the oldest or most senior person at the table to start eating before beginning yourself.

Gift giving: Gifts are often exchanged in Vietnamese culture, especially during holidays and special occasions. When giving a gift, it is a sign of respect to wrap it nicely and present it with both hands. Avoid giving sharp objects, napkins, or anything black, as these are considered bad luck.

Respect for elders: In Vietnamese culture, respect for elders is very important. Be mindful of using respectful language, deferring to their wishes, and avoiding behaviors or actions that may cause them to lose face.

Japanese Etiquette

Japanese etiquette reflects the values and beliefs of Japanese people, which are intended to show respect and consideration for others.

Bowing: Bowing is an important part of Japanese etiquette and is used to show respect and gratitude. The depth and duration of the bow can vary depending on the situation and the status of the person being greeted.

Gift giving: it is often done as a gesture of showing appreciation or respect. When giving a gift, it is customary to use both hands and to wrap the gift in special paper.

Removing shoes: In Japan, it is important to wear clean socks as people remove their shoes before entering a home, temple, or other traditional Japanese buildings. After removing your shoes, remember to place them neatly together facing the entrance.

Silence: Silence is valued in Japanese culture and is often used as a way of showing respect or listening attentively. In some situations, it is considered impolite to speak too loudly or too much.

Eating: Japanese dining etiquette can be quite different from Western dining etiquette. For instant, it is considered polite to slurp noodles and to finish all the food on your plate. It is also customary to say "itadakimasu" before eating and "gochisousama deshita" after finishing a meal.

Business etiquette: In business settings, address people by their titles and to exchange business cards with both hands. It is expected to show respect for hierarchy and to avoid direct confrontation or criticism.

Public transportation: If you are taking public transportation in Japan, it is considered impolite to talk on your phone, eat, or play loud music. It is also customary to give up your seat to elderly or disabled people.

Dubai Etiquette

Dubai is a diverse and multicultural city, and it is essential to be aware of local customs and etiquette when visiting.

Dress modestly: While Dubai is relatively liberal compared to other Middle Eastern cities, it is still a Muslim country, it is essential to respect the local customs. Be mindful to dress conservatively in public places and avoid wearing revealing clothing.

Greetings: It is customary to greet people with a handshake or a slight bow. Men should not extend their hand to women unless the woman initiates the handshake.

Respect Ramadan: During the holy month of Ramadan, it is illegal to eat, drink, or smoke in public during daylight hours. Respect this tradition and avoid eating or drinking in public places during the day.

Public displays of affection: this is not generally accepted in public places.

It is best to avoid public displays of affection.

Alcohol: Alcohol is permitted in Dubai, but it is not allowed in public places. It is only allowed in licensed hotels, bars, and restaurants.

Respect for the royal family and religion: It is essential to show respect for the royal family and Islam, which is the official religion of the UAE. Avoid any criticism of the country, its leaders, or the religion.

Tipping: leaving gratuity is common in Dubai, and it is customary to leave around 10% of the bill.

Language: Arabic is the official language of Dubai, but English is widely spoken. It is always polite to learn a few Arabic words and phrases, such as "salam alaikum" (peace be upon you) and "shukran" (thank you).

Indian Etiquette

India is a country with a rich and diverse cultural heritage. Its etiquette practices vary greatly depending on the region, religion, and social status of the people.

Greetings: In India, it is customary to greet people with a "Namaste" or "Namaskar," which involves bringing your hands together in a prayer-like gesture and bowing slightly. This is a sign of respect.

Dress modestly, covering your arms and legs, especially when visiting religious places. Women should also cover their head if entering a temple.

Remove your shoes before entering a home or a place of worship.

Eating: Indians generally eat with their right hand, and it is considered impolite to use your left hand.

Personal space: Do not be surprised if someone stands very close to you while speaking. Indians tend to stand closer to each other while speaking than in the West.

Punctuality: In India, people have the tendency to be more relaxed about time, so it is not uncommon for meetings to start a little late.

Respect for elders: Elders are highly respected in Indian culture. It is expected that you will stand up when they enter a room and address them with respect.

Public behavior: Public displays of affection are generally not acceptable in India, especially in more conservative areas. It is also considered rude to speak loudly or use foul language in public. Be aware and mindful of others who are praying or meditating.

―――

Desert Region Etiquette

If you are planning to visit a desert region, it is important to be aware of the local desert etiquette.

Dress appropriately: The desert can be extremely hot during the day and chilly at night, so dress in lightweight, breathable clothing and bring layers.

Respect the environment: Desert ecosystems are delicate and vulnerable, so be sure to leave the area as you found it.

Do not litter or disturb the natural landscape, and avoid damaging plants or disturbing wildlife.

Stay on designated paths: Stick to marked trails and paths to minimize your impact on the environment.

Avoid creating new paths or shortcuts, as this can damage the fragile desert terrain.

Pack out what you pack in: Make sure to take all your trash with you when you leave. Do not leave any food scraps or litter behind, as this can attract animals and disrupt the ecosystem.

Be aware of fire hazards: Desert areas can be very dry and prone to wildfires, so be careful with any flames or sparks.

Do not light fires in areas where they're prohibited, and make sure to extinguish any flames completely before leaving.

Respect local customs: If you are visiting a desert region where people live, be respectful of their customs and traditions.

Ask for permission before taking photos or entering private property.

Be mindful of water usage: Water is a precious resource in the desert, so use it sparingly. Do not waste water, and avoid contaminating water sources.

Bring plenty of water, sunscreen, and protective clothing, and let someone know where you are going and when you expect to return.

Be sure to wear sunscreen, a hat, and sunglasses to protect yourself from the sun.

―――

Western Etiquette

Western etiquette refers to the social norms and expectations that govern behavior in Western societies, including those in North America and Europe. Although it can vary depending on the context and setting.

In most Western countries, it is customary to shake hands when meeting someone for the first time or in a professional setting. In more casual situations, a simple wave or nod of the head is acceptable.

When dining in a formal setting, it is important to use utensils correctly, keep your elbows off the table, and wait until everyone has been served before beginning to eat.

(**Hint:** If you are unsure of what to do, follow the lead of your host or hostess.)

Dress appropriately for the occasion or setting. In more formal settings, such as weddings or business meetings, a suit or dress is appropriate. In more casual settings, such as a barbecue or picnic, more relaxed clothing is acceptable.

Be punctual. Arrive on time for appointments, meetings, and social events. If you are running late, it is considered polite to call and let the other party know.

Use polite language, say "please" and "thank you" when appropriate, and avoid interrupting others when they are speaking. Also, avoid using profanity or making inappropriate comments.

It is customary to bring a small gift, such as a bottle of wine, flowers, or chocolates, if you are invited to someone's home for dinner or a special occasion.

Be mindful and respect personal space. Avoid standing too close to others, unless you know them well.

In most Western countries, it is customary to leave gratuity to the service providers, such as wait staff, hairdressers, and taxi drivers. The amount of the gratuity may vary depending on the quality of the service provided.

―――

Spa/Rejuvenation Experience Etiquette

As I was walking into the spa entrance, the soothing fragrance of lemongrass and lavender floating in the air entered my little being in such a magical way, which relieved all of my stressors. I approached the receptionist; she was pleasant and courteous, asked for my name and offered fresh water with a hint of cucumber as I was sitting comfortably on the sofa. Soft piano music in the background, I was thinking to myself "wonderful, how heavenly!" Suddenly I heard footsteps approaching, there were three women coming in, talking amongst themselves with the outdoor-voice. Since they brought some food in paper bags, the receptionist politely let them know it was not allowed to bring outside food to the spa, they started a heated conversation about their right to eat their own food. The manager was then called; she kindly invited them to a private room to continue the discussion. The receptionist then came to me to apologize for the disrupted ambiance.

As I am writing this book, reflecting on that experience, I think it may be useful to add a section about spa experience etiquette, which you may find just simply common sense.

―――

1. Do not bring in outside food and drink. Most spas often have their own menu of refreshments and snacks, and bringing in outside food or drink can be considered rude or disrespectful to the establishment.
2. Arrive on time: Spa staff typically have a tight schedule; a late arrival can throw off their entire day. Be punctual and arrive at least 10-15 minutes before your scheduled appointment to check in, change to spa robe, and relax.
3. Dress appropriately: It is recommended to ask if you should bring the right type of swimwear. Although most spas provide robes and slippers for their guests to wear during their visit. It is important to wear comfortable clothing and avoid wearing any jewelry or accessories that may interfere with your treatment.
4. Communicate your preferences: Let your therapist know if you have any specific preferences or concerns before your treatment. For example, if you prefer a deeper or lighter pressure during a massage, or if you have any allergies or sensitivities to certain products.
5. Use your indoor voice: The spa is a place of relaxation and tranquility, so it is important to keep your voice down and avoid loud conversations.
6. Turn off your phone: To fully disconnect and enjoy the spa experience, it is recommended to turn off your phone or put it on silent mode.

7. Mind your hygiene: It is essential to shower or bathe before using any spa facilities, such as a sauna or hot tub, to ensure good hygiene.
8. Respect others' space: Be mindful of others' personal space and avoid using someone else's belongings or equipment without permission.
9. Leave gratuity appropriately: Tipping is usually not mandatory, but it is a common practice in spas. A typical tip is 15-20% of the treatment price.

———

SPORTS EVENTS

Polo Event Etiquette

Dress appropriately: Polo events are generally formal affairs, so dress accordingly. Men should wear a suit or a blazer with dress pants, while women should wear a dress or a skirt and blouse.

Hats are also common, but make sure to choose one that will not obstruct other people's views.

Arrive on time: Polo matches typically start on time, so arrive early to find your seat and settle in. Latecomers can disrupt the game and other spectators.

Respect the players and horses: Polo players and their horses are the stars of the event, so be sure to give them plenty of space and avoid disturbing them.

Do not enter the field during the game or touch the horses without permission.

Do not walk in front of the spectators: When moving around the field, avoid walking in front of other spectators, especially during a match. Wait until a break in the action or until the end of the chukka (period of play) before moving.

Do not talk during the game: It is considered rude to talk during the match, as it can be distracting to the players and other spectators. Save your conversations for breaks in the action or after the game.

Respect the traditions: Polo has a rich history and tradition, so respect these by standing for the national anthem and removing your hat during the trophy presentation.

Follow the rules of the venue: Different venues may have different rules and regulations, so be sure to follow them to ensure everyone's safety and enjoyment.

Golf Etiquette

Dress appropriately: Wear proper golf attire, which typically includes collared shirts, golf pants or shorts, and golf shoes.

Respect the course: Repair divots, replace divot sand, fix ball marks on the green, and avoid walking on the green when possible.

Be punctual: Arrive on time for tee times, be ready to play when it is your turn, and keep pace with the group in front of you.

Keep quiet: Avoid talking or making noise while others are swinging, and keep cell phones on silent.

Be aware of your surroundings: Watch out for other players on the course, yell "fore" if your ball is headed towards someone, and wait for the group in front of you to clear before hitting.

Be respectful: Shake hands with other players before and after the round, and show good sportsmanship by congratulating other players on their shots.

Follow the rules: Observe the rules of golf, and do not cheat or take shortcuts.

Be efficient: Keep play moving by being ready to hit when it is your turn, and avoid taking excessive practice swings or looking for lost balls for too long.

Take care of equipment: Do not throw clubs, and return rental clubs in good condition.

―――

HOUSEHOLD DAILY

Either you are a guest for a few hours, or sharing a household with other people, be mindful and respectful of your surroundings will ensure a healthy and pleasant environment for everyone.

Living Room Etiquette

Clean up after yourself: If you spill something or make a mess, clean it up right away. It is important to keep the living room tidy and presentable.

Be mindful of noise: If there are other people in the living room, be respectful of their need for peace and quiet. Keep the volume of the TV or music at a reasonable level.

Respect personal space: If you are sitting next to someone, give him or her enough space so they feel comfortable. Do not sit too close or take up more than your fair share of the seating.

Avoid strong fragrances: Avoid wearing or using strong fragrances in the living room, as they can be overpowering and may bother others.

Do not hog the remote: If you are watching TV with others, take turns choosing what to watch and be willing to compromise.

Ask before changing the temperature: If you are feeling hot or cold, ask if it is okay to adjust the thermostat before doing so.

Offer refreshments: If you have guests over, offer them something to drink or snack on. It is a hospitable gesture that can make people feel welcome.

Use coasters: If you are drinking something that could leave a ring on the coffee table or side table, use a coaster to protect the furniture.

Bathroom Etiquette

When using public or shared bathroom, be mindful to:

Keep it clean: Always clean up after yourself. Flush the toilet, throw your paper towels in the trash, and do not leave any personal items behind.

Wait your turn: If someone is already using a stall or sink, wait your turn instead of pushing ahead.

Be considerate: Be mindful of others when using the bathroom. Avoid talking loudly on the phone, playing music or videos without headphones, or engaging in other activities that could disturb others.

Wash your hands: Always wash your hands after using the bathroom, and use soap and water to effectively remove germs.

Use appropriate language: Refrain from using profanity or inappropriate language while in the bathroom. It can make others feel uncomfortable.

Use a reasonable amount of resources: Avoid using an excessive amount of toilet paper, soap, or water. Be mindful of others and try to conserve resources.

Dining Room Etiquette

Wait to be seated: If you are a guest at a dinner party or formal event, wait for the host or hostess to show you to your seat. If you are at a restaurant, wait for the host or hostess to seat you.

Use utensils properly: Start with the utensils farthest away from the plate and work your way in as each course is served.

Hold your fork in your left hand and your knife in your right hand, with the blade facing the plate.

When you are finished with your meal, place your utensils side by side on your plate, with the handles at the bottom right.

Wait for everyone to be served: Do not begin eating until everyone at the table has been served, including the host or hostess.

Use napkins properly: Place your napkin in your lap as soon as you are seated. If you need to leave the table, place your napkin on your chair.

When you are finished with your meal, place your napkin to the left of your plate.

Chew with your mouth closed: It is considered impolite to talk with food in your mouth or to make loud noises while chewing.

Take small bites: Cut your food into small pieces and take small bites.

Do not fill your mouth with food, as this can be unappetizing for others to watch.

Avoid slouching: Sit up straight in your chair and avoid slouching. Keep your elbows off the table while eating; however, it is acceptable to rest your wrists on the edge of the table.

Use polite conversation: Avoid discussing controversial or offensive topics during the meal. Keep the conversation polite, pleasant, and respectful.

Wait for the host or hostess to signal the end of the meal: Do not begin to leave the table until the host or hostess signals that the meal is over.

Thank the host or hostess: Before leaving, thank the host or hostess for the meal and their hospitality.

Kitchen Etiquette

Clean up after yourself: Make sure you clean up any spills or messes that you make, and put away any tools or ingredients that you use.

Do not use someone else's cooking ware without their permission, and return borrowed items promptly.

Respect others' food: Do not take or use food that belongs to someone else without asking first. Similarly, label your own food so others know not to take it.

Be considerate of others: Be mindful of the noise you make while making drinks, cooking and cleaning, especially if it is early in the morning or late at night.

Wash your hands: Always wash your hands before cooking or handling food.

Kitchen towels: take the initiative to replace clean towels when you notice the current ones are soiled.

Last but certainly not least, never leave your dirty dishes piled up in the sink. Put them in the dishwasher or clean them right after use.

Bedroom Etiquette

Respect privacy: If you are sharing a bedroom with someone, respect his or her privacy and personal space.

Knock before entering the room and avoid snooping through their personal belongings.

Keep the bedroom tidy: Keeping the bedroom tidy and organized can create a calm and peaceful environment.

Make sure to clean up after yourself and avoid leaving clutter around the room.

Be mindful of noise: especially at night. Avoid loud conversations or activities that may disturb your roommate or partner.

Respect personal boundaries: Everyone has personal boundaries, and it is important to respect them. Avoid making physical contact with your roommate or partner without their consent.

LUXURY IN YOU

Communicate openly: If you have a roommate or partner, it is important to communicate openly about your needs and expectations. This can help avoid misunderstandings and promote a healthy living environment.

Good hygiene is important in any shared space. Make sure to shower regularly, wash your hands frequently, and avoid leaving dirty clothes or dishes around the room.

———

DINING ADVENTURES

When I am invited to a formal dining event, I always ask for some general information about other guests. Since I want all the guests who will be sharing the table with me to have a positive experience, I have found it pleasantly helpful to lead the conversation for them to talk about their expertise, or to contribute to their subjects of interest at the dining event.

Formal Dining Etiquette

Dress appropriately: Dress formally in a suit or dress. Make sure your clothes are clean and pressed.

Arrive on time: Be punctual and arrive at the designated time.

Wait for the host: Wait for the host to take their seat before you sit down.

Napkin placement: When you sit down, unfold your napkin and place it on your lap.

Use utensils properly: Start from the outside of your place setting and work your way in with each course. Use your utensils from the outside in. When you are not using your utensils, place them on your plate, with the fork tines facing down.

Pace yourself: Eat at a moderate pace, a small bite at a time, and do not finish your meal before others at the table.

Table conversation: Keep conversation light and pleasant. Avoid discussing controversial topics, personal issues, or speaking ill of others.

Drinking etiquette: If wine is served, hold the glass by the stem and not by the bowl. Take small sips and avoid drinking too much.

Thank the host: Thank the host for the meal at the end of the evening.

Things to AVOID at a formal dinner

Do not arrive late: Arriving late can disrupt the seating plan and cause inconvenience to other guests and the host.

Do not use your mobile phone: It is impolite to be distracted by your phone when you should be engaging in conversation with your tablemates. Keep your phone on silent and avoid checking it during dinner.

Do not start eating before everyone is served. Wait for the host to begin eating before you start.

Do not talk with your mouth full: This is a basic rule of table manners that applies to all formal and informal dining situations.

Do not make negative comments about the food: It is impolite to criticize the food or the service, even if you are not enjoying it.

Do not dominate the conversation: Allow other guests to speak and contribute to the conversation.

Do not drink too much alcohol: Drinking too much alcohol can impair your judgment and behavior. Limit your alcohol intake from one to two drinks.

Do not apply lipstick at the dining table. There is a proper place for that activity, which is the restroom.

Remember to be respectful and gracious to your hosts and fellow guests. Use your common sense and good judgment to navigate the formal dinner with ease and poise.

Wine Etiquette

Serving Wine: When serving wine, always hold the bottle by the bottom or the lower part of the neck, not by the cork or the body of the bottle. This will prevent the wine from getting too warm due to the heat of your hand.

Decanting Wine: Decanting wine is often done to aerate and improve the flavor of young red wines. When decanting, pour the wine slowly and steadily, being careful not to disturb the sediment at the bottom of the bottle.

Tasting Wine: When tasting wine, it is important to look, smell, and taste the wine in a specific order.

- First, examine the color and clarity of the wine.
- Next, give it a quick sniff to assess the aroma.
- Finally, take a sip and let it roll around in your mouth to fully experience the flavor and texture.

Toasting: When making a toast, hold your glass up at eye level and make eye contact with the person you are toasting. Be sure to clink glasses gently and only once, and say "cheers" or another appropriate phrase.

Ordering Wine: When ordering wine in a restaurant, it is customary to let the person who is hosting or paying for the meal choose the wine. If you are unsure about what to order, ask the server for recommendations.

Storing Wine: Wine should be stored in a cool, dark place, preferably on its side to keep the cork moist. Avoid storing wine in a place with significant vibrations or temperature fluctuations.

Serving Temperature: Different wines should be served at different temperatures. Generally, white wine should be chilled to around 45-50°F (7-10°C), while red wine should be served at around 60-65°F (15-18°C).

Appetizer Etiquette

Offer to share: If you are at a social gathering with appetizers, offer to share with others, that is a great way to start a friendly conversation.

Use utensils: Use utensils, toothpicks or skewers provided for picking up appetizers. Do not use your fingers.

Take small portions: Take small portions of appetizers so that everyone can have a chance to try them.

Do not double dip: If you are sharing a dip or sauce with others, do not double dip. Use a new utensil each time you dip.

Be considerate of dietary restrictions: If you know someone has dietary restrictions, be mindful of what you are eating in their presence. If possible, offer to bring a dish that caters to their needs.

Wait for the host: Do not start eating the appetizers until the host has invited everyone to begin.

Dessert Etiquette

Dessert is considered a delicacy as it is often associated with luxury, indulgence, and celebrations. It usually involves skillful preparation, making it a special treat for everyone.

Dessert is typically to be offered as the final course of a meal, because it is meant to be savored and enjoyed as a special treat of indulgence.

―――――

Wait until everyone has been served before starting to eat your dessert. It is impolite to begin eating while others are still waiting.

Use the appropriate utensils for the dessert you're served: a fork for cake or pie, a spoon for pudding or ice cream, and a small fork or spoon for desserts like cheesecake or mousse.

MOZA-BELLA

Take small bites and chew with your mouth closed. Take your time to savor each bite. Do not talk with your mouth full.

If you are sharing a dessert, use a clean utensil each time you take a bite. Do not use your own utensil to scoop from the serving dish.

Do not lick your utensils or plate, and avoid scraping the last bits of dessert from the dish with your utensil.

If you are hosting a dinner party, make sure to offer a variety of dessert options to accommodate different dietary restrictions and preferences.

If you are a guest, it is polite to offer to bring a dessert to share. Check with the host beforehand to make sure they are not planning to serve a specific dessert.

————

SPECIAL EVENTS

Afternoon Tea Etiquette

Afternoon Tea is a formal occasion, so it is best to dress up a little. You do not need to wear a ball gown, but a smart outfit will make you feel more elegant and confident.

Wait to be seated: When you arrive, wait to be shown to your seat by your host or the waiting staff. If there are no designated seats, wait for your host to indicate where you should sit.

Use the correct utensils: Afternoon tea usually involves a range of sweet and savory treats, so there may be different utensils for different items. Start from the outside and work your way in as the courses progress. (Hint: The teaspoons should be used for stirring tea only.)

Pour tea properly: When pouring tea, hold the teapot with your right hand and the handle with your left. Pour the tea into the cup, taking care not to spill any.

If you are pouring tea for someone else, be careful not to spill any on their plate or around the area. Ask if they would like milk or sugar before adding it to their cup.

Eat with grace: Take small bites of the food and avoid talking with your mouth full. Pace appropriate time between each bite. Use your napkin to wipe your mouth and fingers, and take care not to drop any crumbs or spill any tea.

Engage in polite conversation: Afternoon tea is a social occasion, so make an effort to engage in polite conversation with your fellow guests. Avoid controversial topics and keep the conversation light and pleasant.

Thank your hosts: After the tea is over, thank your hosts for their hospitality and compliment them on the food and drinks.

It is also a lovely gesture to send a thank-you note or message after the event to express your gratitude.

Cocktail Party Etiquette

A Cocktail party is a social gathering or event where guests are served alcoholic drinks (cocktails), and light refreshments such as hors d'oeuvres, small bites, and finger foods, in a relaxed and casual/informal atmosphere with music in the background.

RSVP: It is an essential courtesy to let your host know if you will be attending or not. This will help the host plan the amount of foods and drinks needed for the party.

Dress appropriately: Cocktail parties can range from casual to formal, so it is important to ask the host the dress code if it is not mentioned on the invitation.

If you are not sure what the dress code is, it is always better to dress more formally.

Wear comfortable shoes as guests usually move around to socialize with one another.

Bring a small gift: It is always a nice gesture to bring a small gift for the host, such as a bottle of wine or a bouquet of flowers.

Be punctual: Arrive on time or within 15 minutes of the start time. It is not polite to show up too early or too late.

Mingle: Cocktail parties are great opportunities to meet and socialize with new people. Make an effort to mingle with other guests. Avoid monopolizing one person's time for too long.

Be respectful: Respect your host's home and belongings, and be courteous to other guests.

Avoid getting too loud or rowdy, and do not overindulge in alcohol.

Offer to help: Ask if the host needs help with anything, such as setting up or cleaning up.

Thank the host: Before leaving, be sure to thank the host for inviting you and for hosting the party.

Ballroom Etiquette

These etiquette guidelines are designed to promote a sense of decorum, respect, and mutual enjoyment among participants in an elegant atmosphere.

Dress appropriately: Dress appropriately for the event, and make sure your attire is clean and well maintained. Men should wear a suit or tuxedo, while women should wear a formal dress with appropriate shoes for ballroom dancing.

Arrive on time: Arrive at the event on time, or even a few minutes early. This shows respect for the host and other guests, and allows you to be settled in before the dancing begins.

Respect personal space: When dancing, it is very important to respect the personal space of other dancers. Make sure you are not stepping on anyone's toes or bumping into them.

Use proper dance floor etiquette: When dancing, stay in your lane and move in a counter-clockwise direction around the dance floor.

Avoid cutting across the floor or dancing in a way that blocks other couples.

Follow the lead: When dancing with a male partner, the female should follow his lead and avoid trying to lead him yourself. This helps to maintain the flow of the dance and ensures that both partners are on the same rhythm.

Practice good hygiene: Make sure you are clean and well-groomed before attending a ballroom event. This includes wearing deodorant, brushing your teeth, and using breath mints if necessary.

Respect the music: When the music starts, it is respectful to be quiet and listen to the music.

Avoid talking loudly or making noise that might distract other dancers.

Last but certainly not least, remember to be polite and courteous to everyone at the event. Say "please" and "thank you" when appropriate, and make an effort to introduce yourself to new people and make them feel welcome.

Concert Etiquette

Arrive on time: which means arrive at least 30 minutes before the show starts to have enough time to find your seat, be settled in, and use the restroom before the show begins.

Dress appropriately: Dress in comfortable and appropriate clothing for the type of concert you are attending. For instance, wear comfortable and casual clothing for a rock concert, and choose more formal attire for a classical music performance.

Silence your phone: Turn off your phone or put it on silent mode during the concert to avoid any interruptions.

Do not sing along: Unless it is an audience participation event, do not sing along or hum to the music, as it may disrupt the experience for those around you.

LUXURY IN YOU

Stay in your seat: Unless it is an audience participation event, do not get up and walk around during the performance, as it can be distracting to others.

Do not talk during the performance: Avoid talking during the performance. If you need to communicate with your company, keep your voice down.

Respect personal space: Try to be mindful of those around you and respect their personal space. Avoid blocking their view or leaning into their space.

Applaud at the right time: It is appropriate to clap and cheer after each piece or at the end of the performance. However, make sure to wait until the piece is over before applauding, as it can be disrespectful to the performer.

Do not bring outside food or drinks: Many venues do not allow outside food or drinks, so make sure to check beforehand. If you are allowed to bring food or drinks, be mindful of the noise and packaging.

Follow venue rules: Follow the venue's rules and regulations, such as no smoking or vaping, no photography, and no recording.

Broadway / Theater Etiquette

Broadway is considered the birthplace of American theater. Its rich history dates back to the late 1700s. It has seen the rise of many iconic performers, directors, and playwrights who have left their mark on the industry.

Broadway shows are popular for their high production values, lavish sets, and elaborate costumes. They are well respected for elevating higher standards of what is possible in live theater, incorporating cutting-edge technology, special effects, and immersive experiences.

———

Dress appropriately: Dressing up a bit for Broadway shows is a sign of respect for the performers and the audience.

Avoid wearing anything too casual, like sweatpants or flip-flops.

Arrive on time: Make sure to arrive at the theater at least 15 minutes before the show starts. Latecomers can be disruptive to the performers and other audience members.

Turn off your phone: Make sure to turn off your phone or set it to silent before the show begins. The sound of a ringing phone can be very distracting.

LUXURY IN YOU

Stay quiet during the show: Refrain from talking, whispering, or making any noise during the show. This includes rustling papers or candy wrappers.

Do not take photos or videos: Taking photos or videos during the show is not allowed and can be distracting to the performers and other audience members.

Wait for intermission to leave your seat: If you need to leave your seat during the show, wait for an appropriate break, such as intermission.

Be respectful of the performers: Show respect for the performers by refraining from booing or heckling, and by applauding appropriately.

Do not sing along or recite lines: While it is tempting to sing along or recite lines during a show you love, it can be disruptive to other audience members and disrespectful to the performers.

Avoid rustling through your bag: Try to have everything you need before the show begins, so you do not have to rustle through your bag during the performance.

Do not bring food or drinks into the theater: Eating or drinking during the show can be distracting to other audience members and disrespectful to the performers.

―――

My Love Message to YOU

So there you have it, my friend. I am sure by now you have already thought of a few other countries that I have not mentioned yet in this book. Therefore, the next page is for you to write. You see, the majority of the book is for you and your journey. This book is meant to record your own journeys, and the memories that you will create as you go on and experience the beauty that life offers. You, my friend, with your inquisitive mind, a respectful soul, and a grateful heart, you will appreciate the unique beauty and its meaning in each fine detail; you will find the joy in experiencing the most simple things in life.

The truth is that luxury is not the exterior factors, it starts from within, and the MOST Luxury has always been in YOU.

———

LUXURY IN YOU

This Event Is:

Date:

Location:

My intention is:

What I learned from this Experience:

The people I noticed and why?

My Inspirational Connections

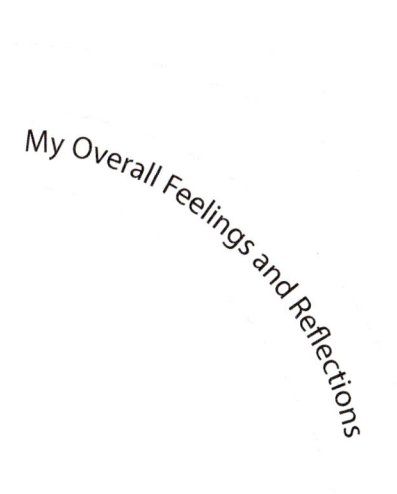

My Overall Feelings and Reflections

LUXURY IN YOU

This Event Is:

Date:

Location:

My intention is:

What I learned from this Experience:

MOZA-BELLA

The people I noticed and why?

My Inspirational Connections

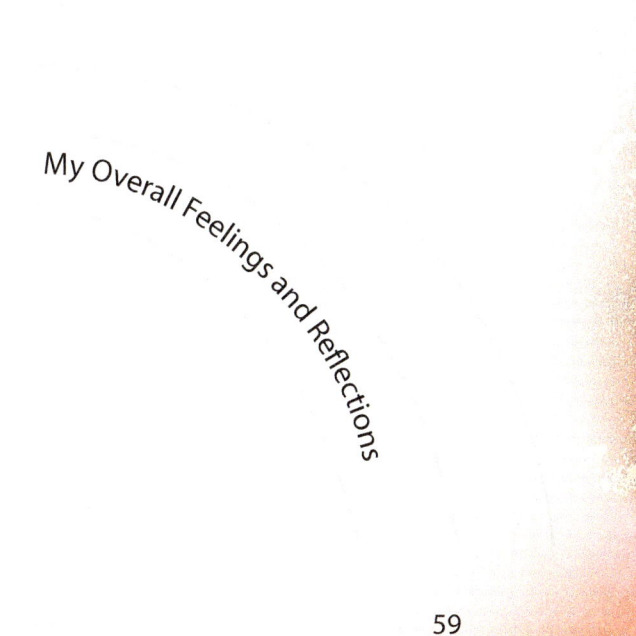

My Overall Feelings and Reflections

LUXURY IN YOU

This Event Is:

Date:

Location:

My intention is:

What I learned from this Experience:

MOZA-BELLA

The people I noticed and why?

My Inspirational Connections

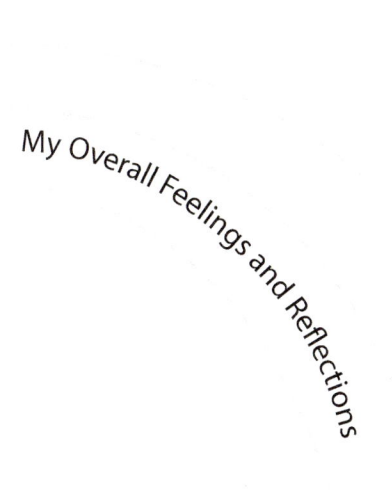

My Overall Feelings and Reflections

LUXURY IN YOU

This Event Is:

Date:

Location:

My intention is:

What I learned from this Experience:

MOZA-BELLA

The people I noticed and why?

My Inspirational Connections

My Overall Feelings and Reflections

LUXURY IN YOU

This Event Is:

Date:

Location:

My intention is:

What I learned from this Experience:

MOZA-BELLA

The people I noticed and why?

My Inspirational Connections

My Overall Feelings and Reflections

LUXURY IN YOU

This Event Is:

Date:

Location:

My intention is:

What I learned from this Experience:

MOZA-BELLA

The people I noticed and why?

My Inspirational Connections

My Overall Feelings and Reflections

LUXURY IN YOU

This Event Is:

Date:

Location:

My intention is:

What I learned from this Experience:

MOZA-BELLA

The people I noticed and why?

My Inspirational Connections

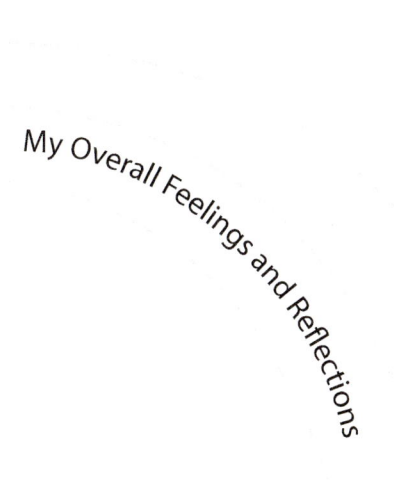

My Overall Feelings and Reflections

LUXURY IN YOU

This Event Is:

Date:

Location:

My intention is:

What I learned from this Experience:

MOZA-BELLA

The people I noticed and why?

My Inspirational Connections

My Overall Feelings and Reflections

LUXURY IN YOU

This Event Is:

Date:

Location:

My intention is:

What I learned from this Experience:

The people I noticed and why?

My Inspirational Connections

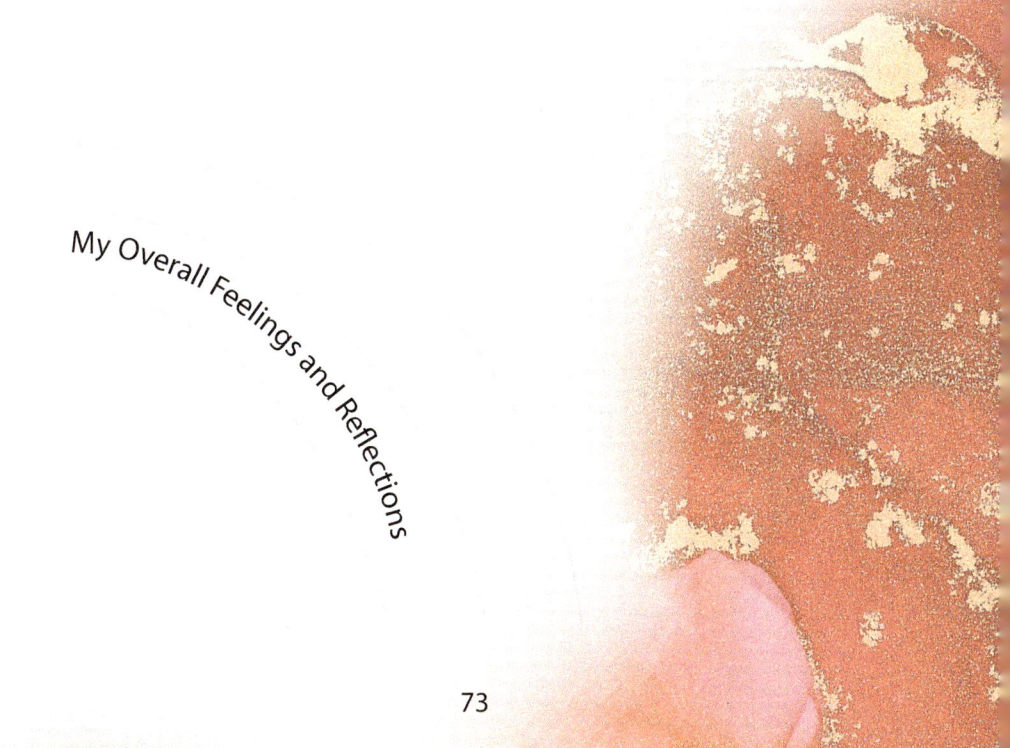

My Overall Feelings and Reflections

LUXURY IN YOU

This Event Is:

Date:

Location:

My intention is:

What I learned from this Experience:

MOZA-BELLA

The people I noticed and why?

My Inspirational Connections

My Overall Feelings and Reflections

LUXURY IN YOU

This Event Is:

Date:

Location:

My intention is:

What I learned from this Experience:

MOZA-BELLA

The people I noticed and why?

My Inspirational Connections

My Overall Feelings and Reflections

LUXURY IN YOU

This Event Is:

Date:

Location:

My intention is:

What I learned from this Experience:

MOZA-BELLA

The people I noticed and why?

My Inspirational Connections

My Overall Feelings and Reflections

LUXURY IN YOU

This Event Is:

Date:

Location:

My intention is:

What I learned from this Experience:

MOZA-BELLA

The people I noticed and why?

My Inspirational Connections

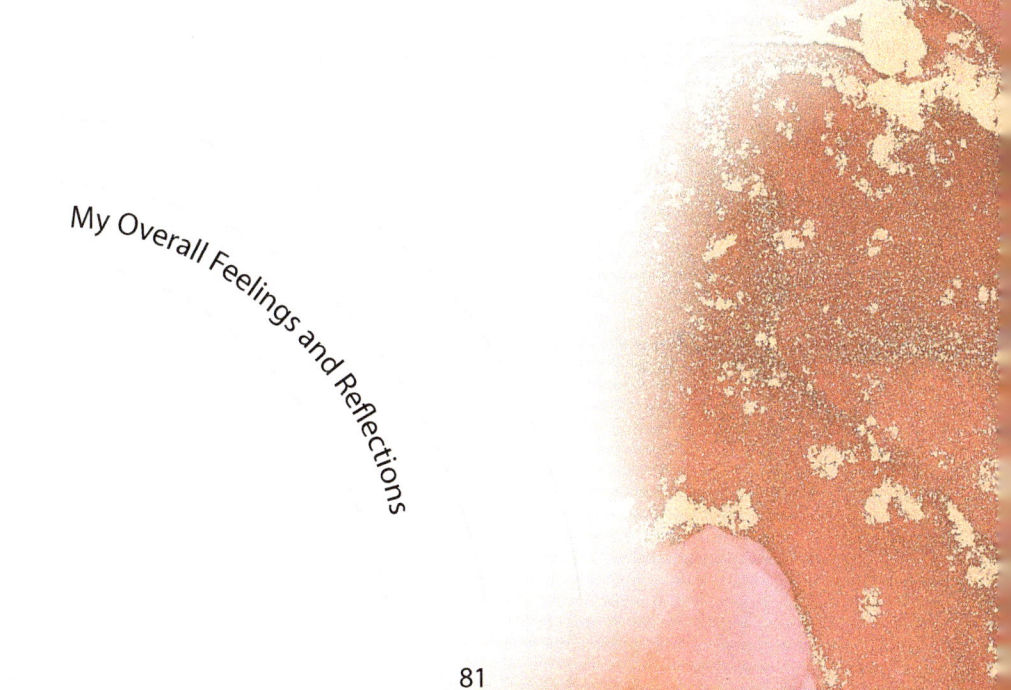

My Overall Feelings and Reflections

LUXURY IN YOU

This Event Is:

Date:

Location:

My intention is:

What I learned from this Experience:

MOZA-BELLA

The people I noticed and why?

My Inspirational Connections

My Overall Feelings and Reflections

LUXURY IN YOU

This Event Is:

Date:

Location:

My intention is:

What I learned from this Experience:

MOZA-BELLA

The people I noticed and why?

My Inspirational Connections

My Overall Feelings and Reflections

LUXURY IN YOU

This Event Is:

Date:

Location:

My intention is:

What I learned from this Experience:

MOZA-BELLA

The people I noticed and why?

My Inspirational Connections

My Overall Feelings and Reflections

LUXURY IN YOU

This Event Is:

Date:

Location:

My intention is:

What I learned from this Experience:

MOZA-BELLA

The people I noticed and why?

My Inspirational Connections

My Overall Feelings and Reflections

LUXURY IN YOU

This Event Is:

Date:

Location:

My intention is:

What I learned from this Experience:

MOZA-BELLA

The people I noticed and why?

My Inspirational Connections

My Overall Feelings and Reflections

LUXURY IN YOU

This Event Is:

Date:

Location:

My intention is:

What I learned from this Experience:

… MOZA-BELLA

The people I noticed and why?

My Inspirational Connections

My Overall Feelings and Reflections

LUXURY IN YOU

This Event Is:

Date:

Location:

My intention is:

What I learned from this Experience:

The people I noticed and why?

My Inspirational Connections

My Overall Feelings and Reflections

LUXURY IN YOU

This Event Is:

Date:

Location:

My intention is:

What I learned from this Experience:

MOZA-BELLA

The people I noticed and why?

My Inspirational Connections

My Overall Feelings and Reflections

LUXURY IN YOU

This Event Is:

Date:

Location:

My intention is:

What I learned from this Experience:

The people I noticed and why?

My Inspirational Connections

My Overall Feelings and Reflections

LUXURY IN YOU

This Event Is:

Date:

Location:

My intention is:

What I learned from this Experience:

MOZA-BELLA

The people I noticed and why?

My Inspirational Connections

My Overall Feelings and Reflections

LUXURY IN YOU

This Event Is:

Date:

Location:

My intention is:

What I learned from this Experience:

MOZA-BELLA

The people I noticed and why?

My Inspirational Connections

My Overall Feelings and Reflections

LUXURY IN YOU

This Event Is:

Date:

Location:

My intention is:

What I learned from this Experience:

The people I noticed and why?

My Inspirational Connections

My Overall Feelings and Reflections

ABOUT THE AUTHOR

Moza-Bella MBA, BA, RN.
Certified 10 X Elite Coach, Speaker, Trainer.

International Speaker. Co-author of Amazon Best Seller "Powerful Female Immigrants". Multi-business owner. Master's degree in Business Administration. Bachelor's degree in Linguistics. Licensed Registered Nurse. Featured on NHK as Peace Ambassador in Japan.

MOZA-BELLA

Moza has helped thousands of professional women get rid of emotional distress and chains, to feel loved and happy, and to achieve the highest level of fulfillment and success.

Moza's passion is to help professional women experience the Freedom of Luxury - the Luxury of being YOU.

Born and raised in Vietnam, living and working in the USA, working in partnership with Grant Cardone to maximize her world-class success program. As a world traveler and speaker, Moza brings the whole world to YOU to enrich your unique beauty and talents.

At Moza-Bella LLC, our clients' amazing intrinsic transformation is our #1 mission.

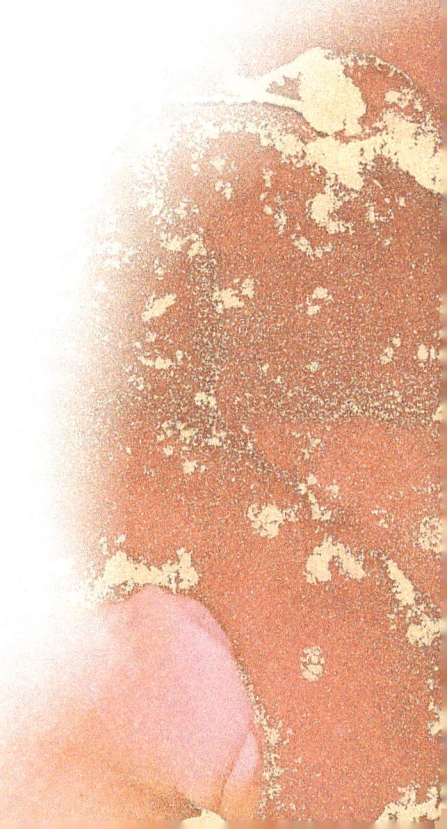

Printed in June 2023
by Rotomail Italia S.p.A., Vignate (MI) - Italy